DINOSAURS

The story of the dinosaurs is a mystery story. Little by little, we have learned some of the secrets of these extraordinary animals over the years. On the way, there have been some big mistakes. When Richard Owen held a dinner for twenty important men in 1853, he hoped that they would remember an unusual evening spent inside the model of an iguanodon. And so they did. But it was only later that people realized that the horn on the iguanodon's nose was really its thumb . . .

We learn more all the time, but there are still more questions to ask. What colour were the dinosaurs? Which was the biggest of all? How fast could they move? And today we have dinosaur books, films, and computer games – what will we think of next? Scientists, businessmen, fossil hunters, kings, children – all kinds of people are interested in dinosaurs. Will that ever end?

OXFORD BOOKWORMS LIBRARY
Factfiles

Dinosaurs

Stage 3 (1000 headwords)

Factfiles Series Editor: Christine Lindop

TIM VICARY

Dinosaurs

OXFORD UNIVERSITY PRESS

Great Clarendon Street, Oxford, OX2 6DP, United Kingdom

Oxford University Press is a department of the University of Oxford.
It furthers the University's objective of excellence in research, scholarship,
and education by publishing worldwide. Oxford is a registered trade
mark of Oxford University Press in the UK and in certain other countries

ISBN: 978 0 19 479446 6

A complete recording of *Dinosaurs* is available on CD. Pack ISBN: 978 0 19 479445 9

Printed in China

Word count (main text): 10,021

For more information on the Oxford Bookworms Library,
visit www.oup.com/elt/bookworms

ACKNOWLEDGEMENTS

Cover image: Getty Images (Skull of Tyrannosaurus Rex/Antonio M. Rosario/Iconica)

Illustrations by: Peter Bull pp.12, 15, 20 (allosaurs and apatosaurus), 38 (maiasaur), Richard
Ponsford p.8/9 (timeline), and size comparisons pp.20, 24, 26, 27, 31, 33, 34, 36, 38, 39

The publishers would like to thank the following for permission to reproduce images: Alamy Images
pp.3 (William Buckland/The Print Collector), 6 (Dinner given by Waterhouse Hawkins/World
History Archive), 19 (Mamenchisaurus dinosaur skeleton/Kim Karpeles), 22 (Pterodactyl flying
dinosaurs/Corey Ford), 27 (Tyrannosaurus Rex/Eye Risk), 32 (Stegosaurus/Stock Illustrations
Ltd); Ardea pp.2 (Ictrhyosaur fossil/Pat Morris), 34 (Parasaurolophus fossil/Francois Gohier);
Corbis pp.0 (Juvenile Dromaeosaur fossil/Mike Segar/Reuters), 7 (Edward Cope/Louie Psihoyos/
Science Faction), 13 (Fossil of Coelophysis/Louie Psihoyos), 24 (Deinonychus sculpture and
skeletons/Louie Psihoyos/Science Faction), 29 (Fossil of Velociraptor attack/Louie Psihoyos),
31 (Triceratops skeleton/Louie Psihoyos), 35 (Rory Chapman/Bettmann), 36 (Fossil of Oviraptor
and eggs/Louie Psihoyos), 41 (Mononykus and Chicken/Louie Psihoyos), 47 (Vintage sketch
of an Iguanodon/Louie Psihoyos/Science Faction), 48 (Dinosaur footprints/Louie Psihoyos),
49 (Bob Bakker/Louie Psihoyos/Science Faction), 52 (Andrew Carnigie/Bettmann); DK Images
p.47 (Iguanodon Teeth/Colin Keates (c) Dorling Kindersley, Courtesy of the Natural History
Museum, London); Getty Images pp.11 (Earth illustrations/Dorling Kindersley), 54 (Girl looking
at dinosaur skeleton/Ron Levine); Kobal Collection p.53 (Jurassic Park/Amblin/Universal); Science
Photo Library pp.2 (Plesiosaur attack/Roger Harris), 3 (Mary Anning), 4 (Gideon Mantell/Paul D
Stewart), 5 (Richard Owen/Royal Institution of Great Britain), 7 (Othniel Charles Marsh/Library
of Congress), 16 (Natural History Museum's Diplodocus/Natural History Museum, London),
26 (Spinosaurus dinosaur/Walter Myers), 33 (Ankylosaur/Roger Harris), 39 (Archaeopteryx fossil/
Jim Amos), 42 (K/T boundary layer of clay and iridium/Prof. Walter Alvarez), 43 (Tyrannosaurus
Rex fleeing from an asteroid strike/D. Van Ravenswaay), 46 (Palaeontological excavation/Pascal
Goetgheluck), 52 (Natural History Museum's Diplodocus, 1905/Natural History Museum)

CONTENTS

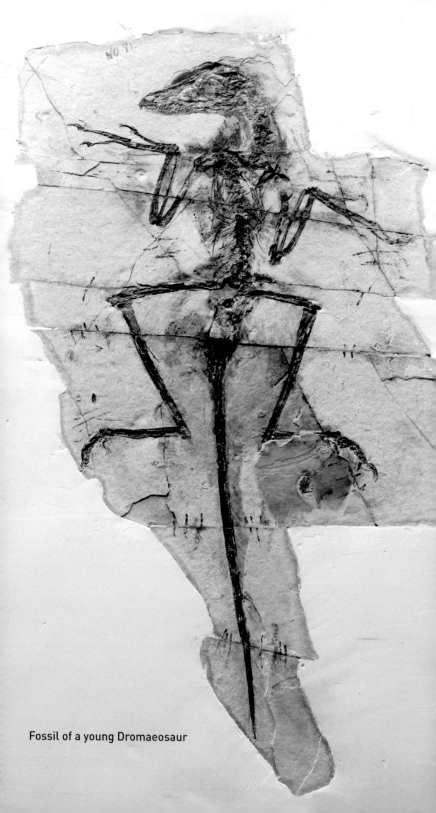

Fossil of a young Dromaeosaur

1 Finding fossils

On a cold winter's day in 1811, a boy and a girl were walking beside the sea in Lyme Regis, south-west England. They were alone, and they walked slowly, looking at the stones under their feet. The sea on their right was still and grey. On their left, near the land, there were a lot of large, broken rocks.

The children were looking for something.

The girl, Mary Anning, was about twelve years old. Every few minutes, she picked up a stone, looked at it carefully, and put it in her bag. Then the boy, her older brother Joseph, began to climb over the broken rocks. It was dangerous; both children knew that. There had been a storm the night before, and some rocks had fallen into the sea. Another big rock could fall at any time.

But the morning after a storm was also the best time to look for fossils – the bones of animals or parts of plants that had become hard and changed into rock.

After a few minutes, Joseph called out to his sister, 'Mary! Quick! Come and look at this!'

When Mary climbed up to him, he showed her a line of teeth, half a metre long, in the broken rock. And behind the teeth, there were some bones, like the head of a strange animal. 'It's a crocodile, isn't it?' Joseph said. 'We've found a crocodile in the rocks!'

Mary looked carefully at the head of the strange animal that Joseph had found.

'What's that round thing?' she asked. 'Look, there, behind the teeth.'

As she cleaned away some sand from the head, a bony circle stared back at them.

'That must be its eye,' Mary said. 'Look – it's almost as big as my head!'

Her brother laughed. 'And its mouth is as big as your body. Be careful, Mary. Look at those teeth! It's going to eat you!'

'Don't be silly,' Mary said. 'It's dead. It died hundreds of years ago. Come on, we've got to find the rest of its body too.'

Some men helped the children to get the bones of the dead animal out of the rock. It was about four metres long, with flat, bony hands and a long tail. It had huge eyes and a long mouth full of sharp teeth. At first, people thought it was a crocodile, but it was not. It was an animal quite different from anything alive in the world today. In 1818, two scientists called Henry de la Beche and William Conybeare gave it the name *Ichthyosaurus*.

Mary Anning was wrong about one thing. The ichthyosaur did not die hundreds of years ago; it died *millions* of years ago, at a time which scientists today call the Jurassic period.

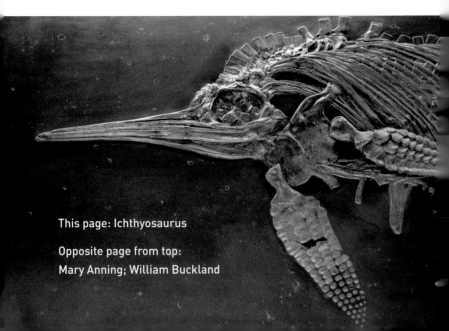

This page: Ichthyosaurus

Opposite page from top:
Mary Anning; William Buckland

But Mary Anning was very clever – she knew how to find the bones of dead animals. All her life, she looked for bones and fossils near her home in Lyme Regis. She found many more ichthyosaurs, and a different sea animal, a plesiosaur. The plesiosaur had a round, flat body, four flat hands, and a very long neck – several metres long – with a very small head at the end of it.

She found a strange flying animal too – a pterosaur. Pterosaurs had long beaks full of sharp teeth and wings made of skin. Some of them had wings as big as the wings of a small plane.

* * *

At this time, in the early 1800s, people were very interested in bones and fossils. Lots of people came to Lyme Regis to see the strange animals that Mary Anning had found. Among them were William Buckland and Gideon Mantell.

William Buckland was a clever scientist from Oxford University. He was very interested in animals, and he liked to watch them and learn about them. In fact, he kept a lot of animals in his house – not just cats and dogs, but snakes, insects, a lot of birds, and a real live bear.

Some of Buckland's ideas were very unusual. He liked to eat animals – but not just the animals that people usually eat, like cows and sheep. He wanted to taste every bird, fish, insect, and animal in the world. So every time he found a new type of animal, he cooked and ate it.

Buckland was also interested in rocks and fossils, and he rode all over England on his old horse, looking for fossils. He often visited Mary Anning in Lyme Regis, and wrote about the ichthyosaurs and pterosaurs. Then one day, in the village of Stonesfield near Oxford, he discovered some fossil bones and teeth. The bones were enormous, and the teeth were sharp, like those of a meat-eater. So, in 1824, Buckland wrote about his animal. He called it *Megalosaurus* – 'big lizard'.

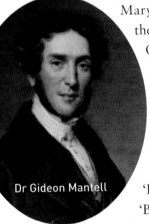

Dr Gideon Mantell

Gideon Mantell was also very interested in Mary's work. He was a doctor who lived in the town of Lewes, in south-east England. One day, in 1822, his wife met some workmen who were using rocks to mend the road near her house. They gave her an interesting rock that they had found. She showed it to her husband when he came home. Dr Mantell was surprised.

'That's not a rock at all,' he said. 'It's a tooth – a fossilized tooth!'

'But look how big it is,' she said. 'What animal does it come from?'

'I don't know,' Dr Mantell said. 'I don't know of any animal with teeth as big as this.'

Dr Mantell went back to the place where the workmen had got the rocks, and found some huge bones there. He decided that the bones and the tooth came from the same animal. But what was the animal like? For three years he wondered about this. He talked to his wife and friends, but he did not tell the world about it. He decided that the tooth was like the tooth of an iguana, a kind of large lizard up to two metres long. But the bones came from an animal much, much bigger – 18 metres long. At last, in 1825, Dr Mantell wrote about his animal, and he called it *Iguanodon*. Later, he sometimes said that he found the tooth, and sometimes that his wife did.

Seven years later, in 1832, Dr Mantell found some bones from a very different animal. This animal, he said, had a very thick skin. He called it *Hylaeosaurus*.

* * *

Another English scientist, Richard Owen, read about these strange animals. Owen knew a lot about bones, and he loved to cut up dead animals, often in his own home. When Owen spent months cutting up a dead rhinoceros, his wife was very unhappy about the terrible smell! In 1842, Owen wrote a book about the animals that Buckland, Mantell, and other people had found. He called his book *Dinosauria* and he was the first person to use the name dinosaur, which means 'terrible lizard'. He said that *Megalosaurus*, *Iguanodon* and *Hylaeosaurus* came from three different groups of dinosaur, and scientists still use these three groups today.

Richard Owen

Dinner in the iguanodon model

Owen was not a very nice man, but he was a great teacher. He wanted everyone to know about the dinosaurs, so he had some models of dinosaurs made for a park in Crystal Palace, in London. The models were as big as real dinosaurs, and you can still see them there today. On 1 January 1853, Owen held a dinner party for twenty-one scientists, *inside* the model of the iguanodon. But Dr Mantell was not there. He had died the year before.

Scientists all over the world read Owen's book. Some of the scientists inside the iguanodon came from Germany and Belgium. They found dinosaurs in their countries too. And in the 1870s, two Americans, Othniel C. Marsh and Edward Drinker Cope, began to find dinosaurs in North America – lots and lots of them.

It was an exciting time in the American West, but it was a difficult, dangerous place to work. There was a lot of fighting everywhere, and the scientists carried guns to defend themselves. But people were building railways, and sometimes the railway builders found bones when they were digging through rocks, so it was just the right place for dinosaur hunters.

Marsh and Cope were not friends; in fact, they hated each other. They hid bones from each other, spied on each other, and sometimes they stole each other's bones too. They argued with each other in newspapers and books. Each man tried to find more dinosaur bones than the other. The fight between them, which went on for about twenty years, was called the 'Bone Wars'.

Marsh won the Bone Wars – he discovered eighty new types of dinosaur, while Cope only discovered fifty-six. But the Bone Wars made dinosaur hunting very popular, and by the time Marsh and Cope died, everyone knew about dinosaurs. Since then, scientists have found dinosaurs in South America, Asia, Africa, India, Europe, and Australia. Some of the most interesting dinosaurs today are the ones that scientists are finding in China. People have even found a few dinosaurs in Antarctica.

In fact, just like people, dinosaurs lived all over the world.

Edward Drinker Cope   Othniel C. Marsh

2   Dinosaur numbers

Everything about dinosaurs is extraordinary. Many of them were big – much, much bigger than humans. The biggest of all, *Argentinosaurus*, weighed more than fifteen elephants. The tallest dinosaur, *Sauroposeidon*, could lift its head 18.5 metres above the ground. That is tall enough to look in through the sixth-floor window of a modern building. The longest dinosaur, *Diplodocus*, was 35 metres long – longer than three buses – and its tail was 21 metres long. The end of that tail could move frighteningly fast – fast enough to knock a man's head off.

Many dinosaurs were very, very dangerous. *Spinosaurus*, for example, was much bigger than an elephant. It had a mouth like a crocodile, but much, much bigger. It had a hundred sharp teeth. An animal like that could probably kill and eat a human in two or three minutes.

Luckily, however, there were no humans alive at the time of the dinosaurs. That is because the dinosaurs lived an

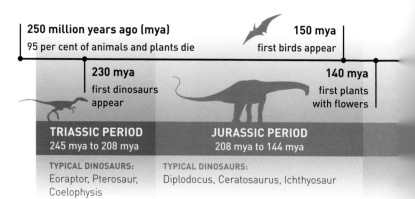

250 million years ago (mya)
95 per cent of animals and plants die

150 mya
first birds appear

230 mya
first dinosaurs
appear

140 mya
first plants
with flowers

TRIASSIC PERIOD
245 mya to 208 mya

JURASSIC PERIOD
208 mya to 144 mya

TYPICAL DINOSAURS:
Eoraptor, Pterosaur,
Coelophysis

TYPICAL DINOSAURS:
Diplodocus, Ceratosaurus, Ichthyosaur

enormously long time ago. It is really hard to understand how long, but it is important to try.

How long have there been people like us – modern humans – on Earth? Well, scientists say that we have been here for about 190,000 years. But before that, there were early humans – people who were almost human, but a little bit different from us. The oldest early human that scientists have found died 3.2 million years ago.

That is a very long time ago. But it is nothing to the time that the dinosaurs lived. The last of the big dinosaurs died 65 million years ago, so all dinosaur bones are *at least* 65 million years old. But many of them are a lot older, of course, because that is when dinosaurs ended. When did they begin?

The first small dinosaur appeared about 230 million years ago. So dinosaurs lived on Earth for 165 million years. That is more than fifty times longer than any kind of humans have lived on Earth.

Look at the timeline on this page. It shows three time periods – the Triassic, the Jurassic, and the Cretaceous. The first dinosaurs appeared during the Triassic period. A lot more dinosaurs appeared during the Jurassic period. And even more dinosaurs lived until the end of the Cretaceous period. Then they all disappeared, very suddenly.

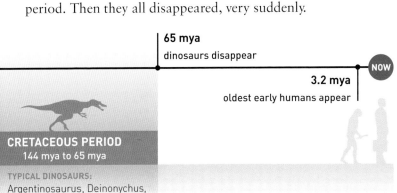

65 mya
dinosaurs disappear

NOW

3.2 mya
oldest early humans appear

CRETACEOUS PERIOD
144 mya to 65 mya

TYPICAL DINOSAURS:
Argentinosaurus, Deinonychus, Baryonyx

3   The first dinosaurs

Because the dinosaurs lived for such a long time, their story is a story of change. Slowly, over 165 million years, the world changed. And the dinosaurs changed too.

The first dinosaurs were not very big or frightening. They looked like small chickens. They ran around on two legs, but instead of wings they had hands with five fingers. They had long tails, small heads, and a mouth with teeth instead of a bird's beak.

In the time before the dinosaurs, there were lots of different animals. But about 250 million years ago, something terrible happened. Thousands and thousands of volcanoes exploded. This made the sky very dark, so it was impossible to see the sun, perhaps for years. Not surprisingly, 95 per cent of all animals and plants died. Only a few kinds of small animals, which did not need much food, stayed alive.

Some of these small animals were called archosaurs. The Earth they lived in was a very different place. There were plants, but no grass, no flowers, and no fruit. And all the continents that we know today – Europe, North America, South America, Asia, Africa, Antarctica – were quite different. All the land was just one large continent, called Pangaea. So these little archosaurs could walk from one side of Pangaea to the other.

In the 1960s, an archosaur called *Marasuchus* was found in Argentina. It was very small, just 10 centimetres high. It ran on two legs and had hands with five fingers. It had a long tail and a mouth with lots of very small teeth, and

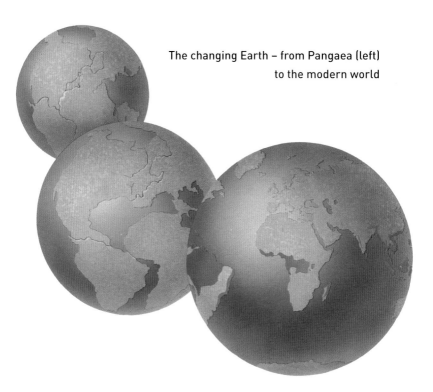

The changing Earth – from Pangaea (left) to the modern world

it probably ate insects and little animals. But it could run very fast. One of the important things about dinosaurs was that they had legs *under* their bodies, like birds. That helped them to run away from enemies like crocodiles, which have their legs *beside* their bodies. It helped them to grow tall too.

Another archosaur was *Eoraptor*, also found in Argentina. It was a little bigger than *Marasuchus*, about 30 centimetres high, like a small dog, and 1 metre long. It also ran on two legs and ate insects and small animals, but it only had three fingers on each hand. It is one of the earliest dinosaurs of all.

These little archosaurs were not the only animals that were alive on Pangaea. There were animals like crocodiles, and there were also small flying animals, like the pterosaurs that Mary Anning found. The pterosaurs had wings made of skin between their fingers. They had long tails and beaks with teeth. They flew all over Pangaea, and sometimes they killed the little archosaurs, and ate them.

Dinosaur family tree

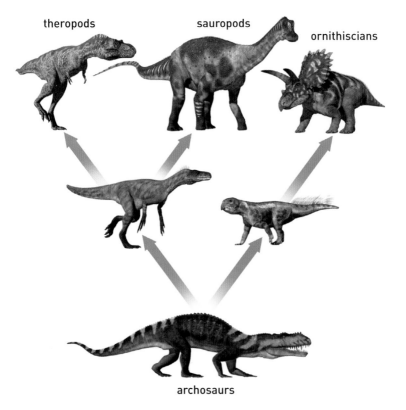

theropods sauropods ornithiscians

archosaurs

All the rest of the world was sea – lots and lots of it. The sea was full of ichthyosaurs and plesiosaurs. These were in the same family as the archosaurs, but they had learned to swim and live in the sea. Some ichthyosaurs were small, but others were huge, more than 15 metres long. They had long mouths full of teeth, and huge eyes to see in the dark.

As millions and millions of years passed, all of these animals evolved in different ways. The small two-legged archosaurs, like *Marasuchus* and *Eoraptor*, evolved over time into the first real dinosaurs. Scientists make a picture,

like a family tree, to show this. In the picture, the oldest
animals – the archosaurs – are at the bottom, and the most
recent dinosaurs are at the top.

Richard Owen, in 1842, said that there were three main
types of dinosaur: meat-eating dinosaurs, and two types
of plant-eating dinosaurs. Scientists today agree with
him. The meat-eating dinosaurs are called theropods. The
plant-eating dinosaurs with long necks and tails are called
sauropods, and the ones with extraordinary thick skins are
called ornithiscians.

One of the first theropods was *Coelophysis*. It ran on two
legs, like *Marasuchus* and *Eoraptor*. But *Coelophysis* was
much bigger, about 1 metre high and 2 or 3 metres long. It
had three strong claws on its hands, and a long tail and long
mouth like a crocodile. It could probably stand up on its back

A coelophysis from Ghost Ranch

legs, as tall as a man. But it was not heavy, because its bones were full of air, like the bones of a bird. It was as long as a small car, but it weighed the same as a seven-year-old child. So it could run very fast, and hunt smaller animals for food.

The first coelophysis was found by an American scientist called David Baldwin in New Mexico in 1881. Baldwin often spent months looking for fossils all alone, in the middle of winter, with only his horse beside him. He sent the bones of the coelophysis to Edward Drinker Cope during the Bone Wars. Sixty years later, in 1947, lots more coelophysis were found at a place called Ghost Ranch, in New Mexico. It is New Mexico's most famous dinosaur.

A very early sauropod was *Thecodontosaurus*, found near Bristol in England in 1836. It was only the fourth dinosaur ever discovered. It was not very tall, but up to 2.5 metres long. It probably walked on two legs, and used its four-clawed hands to help it eat plants and small insects.

A much bigger Triassic sauropod was *Plateosaurus*. *Plateosaurus* was up to 10 metres long and weighed 700 kilograms. It was 3 metres high when it stood on its back legs. This plant-eating dinosaur probably walked on two legs and used the claws on its hands to hold the branches of trees while it ate. The first plateosaur was found in Bavaria in Germany in 1837. It was the first dinosaur found outside England, and the fifth dinosaur to be given a name. Since then, fifty more plateosaurs have been found, in France, Germany, Norway, Switzerland, and Greenland.

An even bigger early sauropod was *Riojasaurus*, found in Argentina. It was up to 2.75 metres high, 11 metres long, and weighed up to 3 tonnes. It needed to eat a lot of plants every day in order to stay alive. And by the end of the Triassic, there were a lot more plants for these dinosaurs to eat.

Dinosaur body parts

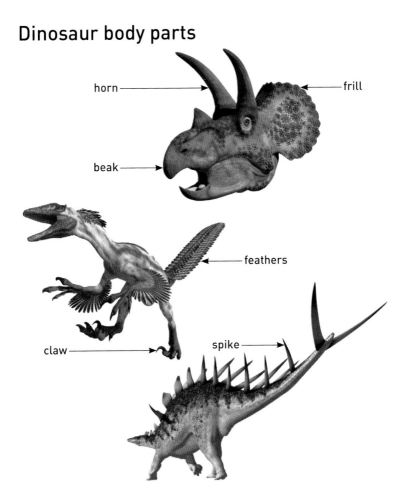

horn

frill

beak

feathers

claw

spike

By the end of the Triassic, the little two-legged archosaurs had evolved into two main types of dinosaurs: the plant-eating sauropods like *Plateosaurus*, and the meat-eating theropods like *Coelophysis*. The third type of dinosaur, the ornithiscians, came later.

But slowly, over millions of years, the Earth continued to change. And as the Earth changed, the dinosaurs changed too. They grew bigger, and stronger – and much, much stranger.

4 Bigger and stronger

As the Triassic period changed into the Jurassic period, the Earth got warmer. And as the Earth got warmer, the dinosaurs got bigger. There was more water in the air, and this helped plants to grow. As the plants grew bigger, there was more food for the animals to eat. So the plant-eating dinosaurs grew bigger and bigger.

The largest Jurassic dinosaurs were the sauropods – the big plant-eaters. They had very big, heavy bodies with long necks and tails. Because their bodies were so heavy, they walked on all four feet. They used their long necks to eat leaves from tall trees, and they used their long, strong tails to defend themselves. They had small heads with very small brains – often about 100 grams, or as big as an orange.

One of the earliest Jurassic sauropods is *Barapasaurus*, which was found in India. It was 18 metres long, and weighed up to 55 tonnes. But that was only the beginning. In the middle and later Jurassic periods, the sauropod dinosaurs began to grow very big indeed.

By the mid-Jurassic, some sauropods could reach leaves that were 10 metres from the ground. The bones in these dinosaurs' necks were hollow in places, so they were not as heavy as other bones. That made it easier to lift these very long necks.

The sauropods' hands still had fingers, which they could use to hold trees and plants, but they mostly walked on four legs. They could not run, because they were too heavy. In some ways, they were like elephants – they probably moved slowly, and they lived in large family groups or herds.

Most big sauropods had at least 100 teeth; some had 600! But even for an animal with so many teeth, some plants were probably hard to eat. Scientists have found stones in sauropod

Diplodocus at the Natural History Museum, London

stomachs; they think that the dinosaurs ate the stones, which then helped to break up the leaves that they ate.

Two of the largest sauropods were *Diplodocus* and *Apatosaurus*. These were found in America in the 1870s by Cope and Marsh. They had small heads, heavy bodies, and big stomachs. They ate a lot of food, and grew very quickly: a young apatosaur probably grew 15 kilograms heavier every day! All these animals had very long, strong tails which they used to defend themselves. *Shunosaurus*, a dinosaur from China, actually had sharp bony spikes on the end of its tail, to hit its enemies with.

Another big Jurassic dinosaur was *Brachiosaurus*, found in the USA and Africa. An adult brachiosaur weighed up to 50 tonnes and was 26 metres long. Unlike most dinosaurs, its front legs were longer than its back legs. This meant that it could lift its huge head, on its long neck, about 16 metres above the ground. On top of its head, between its eyes, *Brachiosaurus* had a big, hollow nose, full of air. Scientists think that it used this nose to make loud noises, perhaps to sing to its friends and frighten its enemies.

Then there was *Mamenchisaurus*, another enormous Jurassic dinosaur from China. This huge dinosaur was 25 metres long. Its neck was 12 metres long – one of the longest necks of any animal ever discovered.

But why were these dinosaurs so big? Well, one reason is that the world was getting warmer and wetter, so there was more plant food for them to eat. But there was another important reason – safety. It is easier for big animals to defend themselves against their enemies. And these big Jurassic sauropods had a lot of very big, dangerous enemies.

One of their most dangerous enemies was *Allosaurus*. *Allosaurus* was a big theropod – a meat-eating dinosaur. It

Mamenchisaurus with its long neck

was about 5 metres high – much taller than a man – and 12 metres long. It weighed 2 tonnes or more. It ran on two legs and had three-fingered hands with long, sharp claws. It had small horns over its eyes, and a mouth full of sharp teeth like kitchen knives. It used these terrible claws and teeth to kill and eat its food. And its favourite food was big sauropods like *Apatosaurus*, *Diplodocus* and *Brachiosaurus*.

But how did it kill these enormous animals? *Allosaurus* was big, but *Apatosaurus* was much bigger – it was one of the biggest animals on Earth. It was 20 to 25 metres long and weighed up to 28 tonnes – more than a family of elephants!

And with its long, strong tail, it could kill a small dinosaur in a second.

Sometimes, perhaps, a brave, hungry allosaur jumped onto the back of an adult apatosaur, and tried to kill it with its terrible teeth and claws. But that was very difficult and dangerous, so perhaps they did it a different way. Some scientists think that allosaurs hunted in family groups. So, perhaps four or five terrible meat-eaters all jumped onto the back of one apatosaur together. That was probably easier, and there was plenty of meat for all of them when they killed it.

And like lions today, they probably did not try to kill the biggest and strongest apatosaur. They looked for an animal that was old, or ill, and killed that. And sometimes they found an animal that was already dead.

But *Allosaurus* was a very good killer. Scientists are sure about that. The dinosaur scientist Thomas Holtz says that dinosaurs like *Allosaurus* changed very little over 100 million years. That means, of course, that they were very successful at what they did. And what they did was hunt, kill, and eat sauropods.

Another terrible Jurassic meat-eater was *Ceratosaurus*. This dinosaur was smaller than *Allosaurus*, but it was still taller than a man. It was 6 to 8 metres long, and heavier than two horses. *Ceratosaurus* also ran on two legs. It had long, sharp claws on its four-fingered hands, and a mouth full of very sharp teeth. It had three small horns on its head and an unusually strong tail. But unlike *Allosaurus*, it did not always hunt big sauropods. The scientist Robert Bakker has found lots of *Ceratosaurus* teeth near the bones of fish and small crocodiles. He thinks that *Ceratosaurus* used its big, strong tail to swim, and hunted for its food in the water.

During the Jurassic period, the continent of Pangaea began to break into two continents, Laurasia and Gondwana. The Atlantic Ocean appeared – at first, it was about fifty kilometres wide. Much of modern Europe was under water then. So there were lots of fish for *Ceratosaurus* to eat in Jurassic seas, lakes and rivers. But there were lots of other animals there too.

A plesiosaur hunting fish

In the Jurassic seas, the ichthyosaurs grew even bigger and stronger. They were hunters, with enormous eyes and long mouths full of sharp teeth – and they could swim very, very fast, probably at 30 to 50 kilometres per hour.

There were plesiosaurs in the sea too. Plesiosaurs did not look like fish: they had round, flat bodies, with four huge, flat hands that they used to push themselves through the water. They had short tails but very long necks, sometimes over 10 metres long. Some had very small heads, but others had huge heads, 3 metres long, bigger than any other dinosaur head.

In the Jurassic skies, a new type of pterosaur appeared – the pterodactyl. Pterodactyls had longer necks than Triassic pterosaurs, and they had bigger brains too. Most of them had long mouths full of sharp teeth, and many of them ate fish. Most pterodactyls were as big as large birds today, but a few were much, much bigger. In fact, the largest pterodactyl of all – *Quetzalcoatlus* – had wings 12 metres wide: bigger than a small plane.

But *Quetzalcoatlus* lived in the Cretaceous period, which came after the Jurassic. It was in the Cretaceous that dinosaurs grew *really* big.

Two pterodactyls flying high

5 Big, bad, and dangerous

During the Cretaceous period, Pangaea, which was once a single continent, continued to break into smaller parts. The Earth began to look more like the world today: several different continents, with large seas between them. This meant that, as time passed, different dinosaurs evolved in each continent. The dinosaurs of China, for example, were different from those of South America.

But in every continent there were large, plant-eating sauropods. They grew even larger because the Cretaceous world was warmer and wetter than before, so plants grew bigger and stronger. And for the first time, some plants had fruit and flowers. So there was a lot more food for the big dinosaurs to eat.

The biggest dinosaur of all was probably *Argentinosaurus*. This enormous animal was between 33 and 41 metres long, 6 to 7 metres high, and weighed between 75 and 90 tonnes. That is more than several families of African elephants. To keep its huge body alive, one argentinosaur probably needed to eat two or three large trees every day. There were probably thousands of these enormous animals in South America, so just think about the number of trees that were eaten every day!

It is hard to understand how any enemy could kill *Argentinosaurus*. It was just too big. Most meat-eaters probably just waited for it to die, and ate it then. But there were plenty of large, meat-eating dinosaurs in the Cretaceous. Perhaps from time to time some of them did try to kill a baby argentinosaur, or a sick or old animal. If they tried to kill a healthy adult they probably got hurt or killed.

* * *

Not all of the terrible killers in the Cretaceous were big. In 1964, John Ostrom, a scientist from Yale University in America, discovered *Deinonychus*. This animal was too small to kill *Argentinosaurus*, but it was still very dangerous. It was about 3 metres long, as tall as a man, and probably covered in feathers like a bird. It had a big brain, and a mouth as long as a man's leg, full of sharp teeth. Its hands had three fingers with long, sharp claws, and on the second toe of its back feet there was another big, dangerous claw.

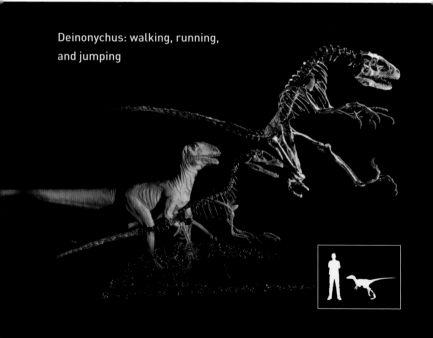

Deinonychus: walking, running, and jumping

Deinonychus weighed about 80 to 100 kilograms, and it could run very fast. Scientists think that *Deinonychus* hunted in groups, like lions today. When they found a large, plant-eating dinosaur, five, ten, or even twenty deinonychus jumped onto it, all together. They bit it with their sharp teeth, and cut it with their terrible sharp claws, until it died. Then they ate it.

Deinonychus was very frightening, but *Utahraptor* was even more dangerous. It had terrible teeth and claws like *Deinonychus*, but it was much bigger. It was 6 to 7 metres long, taller than the tallest horse, and it weighed up to 1.1 tonnes. It had a big brain too, so it was probably very clever. And just like *Deinonychus*, these dinosaurs hunted together in groups. For plant-eating dinosaurs, this was like a really bad dream. They could look up, and see not one, but five or ten terrible killers running towards them, very fast. It was usually the last thing they ever saw.

However, *Utahraptor* was not the biggest killer. In 1983, an Englishman called William Walker discovered an enormous fossil in Surrey, near London. He called it *Baryonyx*, which means 'heavy claw'. This dinosaur was much bigger, and so a lot slower, than *Utahraptor*. It weighed up to 5.4 tonnes, it was 13 metres long, and 2.5 metres high. It had strong, sharp claws on its three-fingered hands, and a long mouth like a crocodile.

We know that *Baryonyx* ate meat, because inside its stomach scientists found the bones of an iguanodon, and a lot of fish bones too. *Baryonyx* probably lived near water, and used its big, sharp claws and its long crocodile mouth to catch fish, like some North American bears today.

An even bigger meat-eater than *Baryonyx* was *Spinosaurus*, which was found in Africa by Ernst Stromer,

a German scientist. *Spinosaurus* looked like *Baryonyx*, but it was much, much bigger. It had a long crocodile mouth, sharp claws on three-fingered hands, and a huge sail on its back. It weighed 8 to 13 tonnes, as much as the biggest African elephant. It was 14 to 18 metres long and 3 metres tall. A spinosaur head that was discovered recently was 2 metres long – longer than a tall man.

All these dinosaurs were terrible. But the most famous and terrible of all the meat-eating theropods is *Tyrannosaurus rex*. This animal was also enormous. It weighed 6 to 7 tonnes and it was over 4 metres tall – taller than *Spinosaurus*. Unlike most dinosaurs, it had very small arms and hands, so it probably used its mouth to kill and eat things. But this was no ordinary mouth – it had over 50 teeth, some as big as a large banana. And its jaws were extraordinarily strong – much stronger than the jaws of a lion or a bear.

So just how strong were those jaws? What is there in the modern world that is like them? Recently, scientists measured the 'bite' of a modern machine which picks up old cars and breaks them into small pieces. Then they measured the bite of the jaws of a tyrannosaur – and it was 50 per cent stronger than the machine. So a tyrannosaur could easily bite right through a car – in a world with both tyrannosaurs and cars, of course!

Tyrannosaurus rex

Because they were so big, tyrannosaurs could probably not run very fast. So some scientists think that they did not hunt like *Deinonychus*; they just found dead animals and ate them. But other scientists disagree. They say that really big sauropods, like *Diplodocus* and *Argentinosaurus*, could not run fast either. And scientists have found damage from tyrannosaur teeth on the bones of two dinosaurs which escaped. This shows that tyrannosaurs tried to kill living dinosaurs.

Tyrannosaurus was a North American dinosaur: in Hell Creek, Montana, scientists have found fossils from more than fifty tyrannosaurs. But in China and Mongolia, they have discovered fossils of *Tarbosaurus*, a dinosaur in the same family as *Tyrannosaurus*. *Tarbosaurus* also had small hands, and big jaws full of sharp teeth. It had a large brain, and it could smell and hear well, which helped it to hunt. Perhaps it also had feathers around its neck.

Velociraptor is a much smaller theropod from China and Mongolia. The first velociraptor was found in the Gobi Desert in 1922, by an American called Roy Chapman Andrews. It was a small dinosaur, 2 metres long and about 60 centimetres tall, and it was covered in feathers. *Velociraptor* did not weigh much – 15 to 18 kilograms, which is less than a large dog. But unlike a dog, it ran on two legs, and had hands with three sharp claws. And like *Deinonychus*, it had another very long, sharp claw on each foot. *Velociraptor* probably ran very fast and hunted in groups, like *Deinonychus* and *Utahraptor*. Like them, it was a very frightening killer.

But even the most terrible killer can get things wrong sometimes. In the Gobi Desert in 1971, scientists discovered two extraordinary fossils. One was a velociraptor, the other was a plant-eating dinosaur called protoceratops.

The two dinosaurs had died when they were trying to kill each other. The protoceratops had the velociraptor's right arm in its jaws. It was trying to bite its arm off. The velociraptor had its claws in the head and neck of the protoceratops. It was trying to cut the protoceratops's neck open.

This terrible fight happened beside a hill of sand. As the two dinosaurs were fighting, the hill fell on top of them. So they both died. And there they stayed, for millions of years, under the sand, until one day the scientists found them.

But what about *Protoceratops?* What type of dinosaur was that?

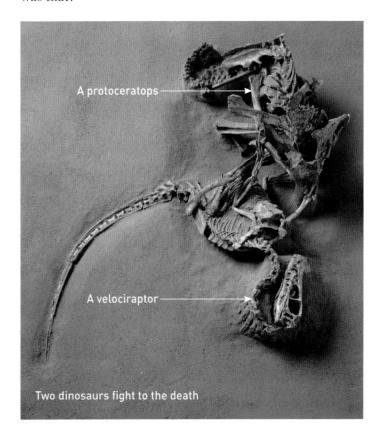

A protoceratops

A velociraptor

Two dinosaurs fight to the death

6   Strangest

Protoceratops is one of the third type of ornithiscians. The ornithiscians are the st dinosaurs. They were plant eaters, but man horns, and they defended themselves with th strong skin.

There were very few ornithiscians in the Triassic period. They began to appear in the Jurassic, and there were lots of them in the Cretaceous. *Protoceratops* was a very successful small dinosaur. Its mouth was like a bird's beak and had a very strong bite. And behind its head, *Protoceratops* had a large frill of skin. This frill was probably brightly coloured, and the dinosaur used it to frighten its enemies and attract females.

Triceratops was like *Protoceratops*, but much bigger. In fact, *Triceratops* was huge: it was 8 metres long, and weighed 11 tonnes, much more than the largest African elephant.

Like *Protoceratops*, it had a mouth like a bird's beak, and a large frill of skin and bone behind its head. Its head was enormous, and it had three large horns. *Triceratops* used these horns to defend itself against its enemies. We know that this happened because some *Triceratops* horns have damage from *Tyrannosaurus* teeth on them.

The ornithiscians had many ways to defend themselves against enemies like *Tyrannosaurus*. *Huayangosaurus*, found in China in 1982, had lots of sharp spikes all along its back. There were bony spikes on its shoulders too, and on the end of its tail. *Stegosaurus*, from North America, was much the same. These dinosaurs used their strong, bony tails to

Triceratops

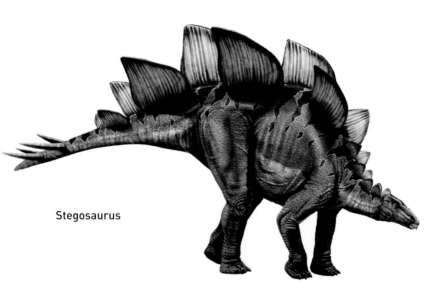

Stegosaurus

hit their enemies. Several meat-eaters, like *Allosaurus*, have been found with holes in their bones made by the spikes on the tail of a *Stegosaurus*.

Animals like these from the late Jurassic have been found in Europe and Africa. All of them were huge, as big as a modern rhinoceros.

Ankylosaurus lived in the late Cretaceous. It had a really thick skin, with spikes all over its back, head and sides. It had a very strong tail with a heavy club at the end, which was excellent for fighting enemies. *Ankylosaurus* was up to 9 metres long, and weighed up to 8 tonnes – much more than an elephant. So when that tail hit something, it hurt.

Tenontosaurus was another big, plant-eating animal, but it was not as strong or dangerous as *Ankylosaurus*. It lived in large herds in North America; in fact, some scientists call it 'the cow of the Cretaceous', because there were so many of them. *Tenontosaurus* was an everyday food for meat-eating hunters like *Deinonychus*.

Iguanodon was an ornithiscian too. It lived in large family groups or herds, like cows or sheep today; in Belgium, the fossils of forty of them were found in the same place. *Iguanodon* had a long face like a horse, with a mouth like a beak for eating plants. It could eat plants well, moving both jaws at once (we humans only move the bottom jaw). *Iguanodon* sometimes walked on two legs, and sometimes on four. Each hand had a sharp spike, like a thumb, which it used to fight its enemies, and it could also pick things up with the help of its little finger. It was as big as a large African elephant.

Hadrosaurs were in the same family as *Iguanodon*, but they were even stranger. These plant-eating dinosaurs had flat, wide beaks with teeth inside them – lots of them. In fact, some hadrosaurs had up to 720 teeth (humans only have 28). New teeth were growing all the time to take the place of any teeth that fell out.

Hadrosaurs had long faces like horses too, and they lived in large herds all over North America. The smallest was as big

Ankylosaurus

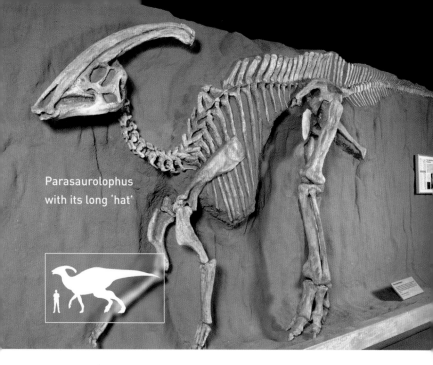

Parasaurolophus with its long 'hat'

as a horse, but many were bigger than elephants. One of the strangest hadrosaurs was *Lambeosaurus*. It was 3 or 4 metres high, and weighed up to 8 tonnes. On its head was a large bone, like an enormous hat. The 'hat' was as big as a man.

The male *Parasaurolophus* had an even bigger 'hat' on the back of its head. This 'hat' was really a long, hollow bone, about 1 metre long, joined to its nose. At first, scientists could not understand this. What was it for? Then they found a possible explanation. When they blew air through this long, hollow bone, it made loud musical sounds.

Was *Parasaurolophus* a musical dinosaur? It is quite possible. The males could make wonderful sounds with these long, hollow bones on their heads. Perhaps they did this to attract the females, or to call to their children. They probably did it when they saw an enemy. And maybe sometimes they did it just for fun, because they liked singing to each other.

But the hadrosaurs were interesting for another reason – their family life.

7 Family life

In 1923, the American scientist Roy Chapman Andrews discovered something very strange. In the Gobi Desert, in Mongolia, he found the bones of a new dinosaur. It was about 2 metres long, with a strong beak, no teeth, and a thin 'hat' on top of its head. And it was probably covered with feathers, like a very big chicken.

Underneath this dinosaur there was a nest full of eggs. This was the first time anyone had found dinosaur eggs. At first, Roy Chapman Andrews thought that the eggs belonged to a different dinosaur, *Protoceratops*. The new dinosaur, he thought, was trying to steal them when it died. So he called his new dinosaur *Oviraptor*, which means 'egg stealer.'

Roy Chapman Andrews
with dinosaur eggs

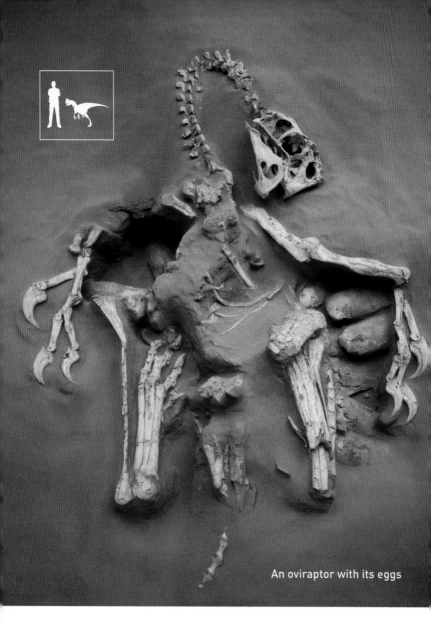

An oviraptor with its eggs

But later, in the 1990s, another oviraptor was found on a nest of eggs. Scientists looked at these eggs very carefully, and decided that the eggs did not belong to *Protoceratops* after all – they belonged to *Oviraptor*. The female oviraptor was sitting on her own eggs when she died. She was keeping them warm with her body, like a bird.

This was a surprise. At this time, nobody thought that dinosaurs could be good parents. Most scientists thought that dinosaurs just laid their eggs on the ground, and walked away. But the oviraptor was taking care of her eggs like a good mother.

Most dinosaurs could not do this. They were much too heavy to sit on their eggs. In Montana, scientists found hundreds of dinosaur nests, but the eggs in the nests came from a type of hadrosaur that weighed 3 tonnes. Were these mothers interested in their babies? Probably not, the scientists thought. They probably just laid their eggs, and forgot all about them.

But there was a problem. They found a lot of baby dinosaurs in the nests beside the eggs. These baby dinosaurs were very small, no bigger than a chicken. They could not walk far, because their bones were not strong enough. But their teeth showed that they had eaten plants. How did the baby dinosaurs find these plants, when they were too young to walk?

The scientists thought hard about this. The baby dinosaurs did not find the plants, they decided. That was impossible; they could not walk. So it must be the *parents* who found the plants. They brought them to their nests, for their children to eat. These dinosaurs were looking after their children, like good parents. So the scientists called this new dinosaur *Maiasaura*, which means 'good mother lizard'.

Maiasaurs laid twenty or thirty eggs in each nest. Then they covered the eggs with dead plants, to keep them warm. When the babies came out of the eggs, they weighed about 1 kilogram, but they grew very quickly. Ten years later, they were adults, weighing 3 tonnes. This shows they were warm-blooded, because cold-blooded animals cannot grow that fast.

When they could walk, baby maiasaurs followed their parents around, looking for food. Maiasaurs were very successful: in one fossil site, there are over 10,000 animals. They lived in huge herds, like many animals in Africa today. And all around them, like lions in Africa, were the hunters – tyrannosaurs, deinonychus, utahraptors. When the baby maiasaurs saw them, perhaps they ran under their parents' legs, to stay safe.

Tyrannosaurs probably fed their babies too – but with meat, not plants. As the young tyrannosaurs grew, they probably hunted together in groups. Young tyrannosaurs had long legs, but they were not heavy, so they could probably run much faster than their parents. Perhaps the adults and children hunted together, the young tyrannosaurs chasing an animal towards their enormous parent. Or perhaps the young hunted the smaller animals, and their parents hunted the big, slow-moving ones. Tyrannosaurs did not always kill their food, of course. Sometimes they just found it lying on the ground. And a dead dinosaur was a free meal for all the tyrannosaur family.

8 Birds

In 1861, a small fossil was found in Germany. It was very small – no bigger than a chicken. Its bones looked like those of *Compsognathus*, a small theropod dinosaur which was found in the same place ten years earlier. But this new fossil's arms and legs were covered with feathers. Scientists called it *Archaeopteryx*.

When the English scientist T. H. Huxley looked at *Archaeopteryx*, he noticed something else. Its bones were hollow, just like the bones of birds. There was a lot of air in them, so they did not weigh very much. *Archaeopteryx*, like *Compsognathus* and most theropods, ran on two legs. And because *Archaeopteryx* had feathered wings, it could probably fly. This gave Huxley an idea: perhaps birds evolved from theropods.

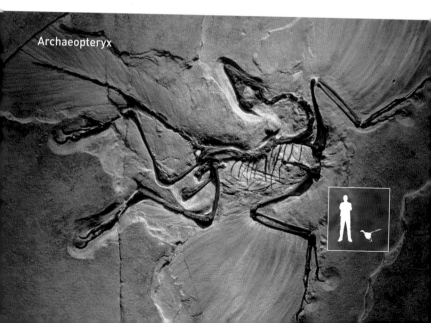

Archaeopteryx

For the next hundred years, scientists argued about this. It is a crazy idea, some people said: how can a dinosaur like *Tyrannosaurus* be in the same family as the birds we see in our gardens?

But then, in 1964, the American scientist John Ostrom discovered *Deinonychus* in Montana, USA. *Deinonychus* was a theropod, like *Tyrannosaurus*, but its bones were like those of birds. It could move its wrists and arms in the way a bird does, and its bones were hollow. *Tyrannosaurus* also had some hollow bones, and so did the big sauropods like *Diplodocus* – that is why its enormously long neck and tail are not as heavy as they look. So Ostrom decided that Huxley's idea was right.

In 1996, scientists in China made another extraordinary discovery – a small dinosaur called *Sinosauropteryx*. It was very like *Compsognathus*, but there was an important difference: *Sinosauropteryx* had feathers all over its body. The sand where it had died was very fine and soft, so scientists could see that it had had feathers. *Sinosauropteryx* was a theropod, like *Tyrannosaurus*, but it was covered in feathers like a bird.

No other animals have feathers – only dinosaurs and birds.

In the next few years, Chinese scientists discovered many more feathered dinosaurs. The one most like a bird was *Microraptor*, which had a long tail, a beak with small teeth, and claws on its hands and feet. It was smaller than *Archaeopteryx*, but it also had long feathers on its arms and legs. So perhaps it flew with four wings, not two.

Other Chinese dinosaurs, like *Oviraptor*, had feathers but could not fly. So which came first – feathers or flying?

Today, scientists think that many dinosaurs had feathers.

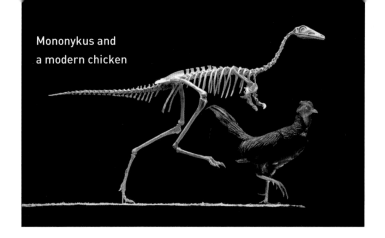

Mononykus and
a modern chicken

The feathers kept the dinosaurs warm. They also helped dinosaur mothers, like *Oviraptor*, to keep their eggs warm in their nests. So the feathers probably came first.

Much later, some small feathered dinosaurs, like *Microraptor* and *Archaeopteryx*, probably learned how to climb into trees. They used their claws and beaks to help them climb. They slept in the trees at night, safe from their enemies. In the morning, they came down from the trees. As they came down, they sometimes opened their wings and jumped. This helped them to fall down more slowly.

Over millions of years, they learned to do this better. Sometimes, when they jumped from trees, they were able to catch small animals by surprise. Those with the best wings and feathers caught more food, so they lived longer, and had more children. Some of their children were born with better wings and better feathers. And one day, they learned to fly.

Even dinosaurs which could not fly, like *Oviraptor*, were like birds in other ways. They laid eggs in nests, and sat on the eggs to keep them warm. And dinosaurs like *Maiasaura* brought food to their babies in the nests, like birds. Even *Tyrannosaurus* probably had feathers around its neck, and hollow bones with air in them. *Tyrannosaurus*, in fact, was not very different from an enormous, terrible chicken!

Dinosaur scientists are very sure about this. Thomas Holtz says it clearly: 'Birds *are* dinosaurs.'

9 A sudden end

Birds, of course, are still with us. But all the other dinosaurs disappeared, 65 million years ago. Why? What happened?

Scientists wondered about this for a long time. Dinosaurs, after all, were very successful animals indeed. They had lived on Earth for 165 million years, and they were the biggest, strongest, and most successful animals of all time. In the late Jurassic and Cretaceous periods, there were dinosaurs all over the Earth. They lived on every continent – even in Antarctica, which was much warmer at that time than it is today. And then, 65 million years ago, they all disappeared, very suddenly. There are no dinosaur fossils anywhere on Earth from after that time. Something terrible must have happened to them. But what was it?

In the 1970s, a scientist called Walter Alvarez tried to answer this question. He looked at the rocks from the Cretaceous, and the time after that – the Tertiary. There were hundreds of dinosaur fossils in the Cretaceous, and none in the Tertiary. But in between the Cretaceous and the Tertiary, he found a thin line of clay, a kind of soft, wet rock.

The dark clay line containing iridium

He found this line of clay all over the world, and everywhere it was the same. In it, he found a silver-white metal called iridium. Iridium is very unusual on Earth, but there is a lot of it in meteors – the rocks that sometimes fall onto the Earth from the sky. So the iridium came from a meteor, Walter Alvarez said – a meteor that hit the Earth 65 million years ago.

We know it was a big meteor, Alvarez said, because there is so much iridium everywhere. He thought that the meteor was a rock between 10 and 15 kilometres across, which hit the Earth with an enormous BANG! It made a crater – a very big hole in the ground – that was 160 kilometres across. A huge ball of fire destroyed anything near the crater, and the ground shook violently. In the sky, dark clouds hid the sun for months, perhaps years.

The meteor falls to Earth

Without sunlight, almost all the plants on Earth died. The big plant-eating dinosaurs – like *Argentinosaurus* – soon died, because they had nothing to eat. The meat-eating dinosaurs, like *Tyrannosaurus*, lived a little longer, because there were lots of dead plant-eaters to eat. But then the meat went bad, and there was nothing left to kill. So they died too.

Well, it is an interesting idea, people said, but where is this crater? A hole in the Earth, 160 kilometres across – that cannot be difficult to find. Why has nobody seen it?

Walter Alvarez looked for this big crater, and with the help of a scientist called Glen Penfield he found it. There was a reason why nobody had seen it before: it was under the ground, in the Yucatan Peninsula of Mexico. In the past 65 million years, the rocks had moved and covered it up, but it was still there. It measured 180 kilometres from one side to the other, which was even bigger than he had expected. He called it the Chicxulub crater.

So scientists think the Age of the Dinosaurs ended like this. One day, 65 million years ago, the world was full of dinosaurs. It began like any other day. Huge herds of dinosaurs were walking slowly across Mexico. Oviraptors were sitting on their nests, and maiasaurs were finding food for their babies. Small feathered dinosaurs were flying from trees. Huge stegosaurs were walking slowly through the forest, and argentinosaurs were eating the tops of trees. Tyrannosaurs were watching the plant-eaters carefully, hoping for a meal. And dinosaurs from the parasaurolophus family, with their strange, hollow heads, were singing to their friends far away.

The plant-eaters kept their eyes open, as they did every day. They were looking for danger – for tyrannosaurs and utahraptors, the enemies that wanted to kill them.

But none of them looked up into the sky, where the real danger was.

Then, suddenly, in a few seconds, it happened. A bright light filled the sky, and there was an enormous BANG! – louder than anything they had ever heard. A great wind knocked all the trees flat, and a few seconds later, everything in the forest was on fire.

All the dinosaurs nearest to the meteor were burned in a few minutes. There was nothing left of them, nothing at all. Those more than 50 kilometres away died more slowly. But all of them, all over the world, began to die.

In a few seconds, 165 million years had ended.

Not everything died, of course. Some small animals, like insects, snakes, and small birds, lived. Because they were not very big, they did not need much food. One of these small animals looked a bit like a mouse. It was a warm-blooded animal, covered in soft hair, and it probably lived in holes in the ground. Dinosaurs ate lots of them every day – but now, suddenly, the dinosaurs were gone. So now this animal could come out of its holes, and feel a little bit safer.

This small, unimportant animal was an early mammal. Over the next 64.5 million years, it slowly evolved into many different types of mammals – elephants, lions, bears, horses, sheep, and humans.

And today there are mammals all over the Earth, just as, once upon a time, there were dinosaurs.

10   Studying dinosaurs

But how do we know all this? There were no humans alive when the dinosaurs lived, and we cannot travel back in time to watch them. So how do we know?

We can learn a lot about dinosaurs from fossils. There are two types of dinosaur fossils: body fossils, and trace fossils.

Body fossils are what is left of the real bones from dinosaur bodies. Over time they have changed and become hard, like rock. Sometimes scientists are lucky, and find all the bones of a single dinosaur in one place, but that is very unusual.

Scientists measure a
fossil bone in France

Mantell's drawing of an iguanodon, with fossil teeth

Usually, they just find a few bones, and the other parts of the body have disappeared. This may be because when the dinosaur died, some other animals ate it, and carried away the bones. Sometimes water has washed some of the bones away, or the rocks that contained the fossils have broken into smaller pieces.

But even from one fossil, we can learn a lot. Dr Mantell learned a lot from the single iguanodon tooth he found in 1822.

It was very big, so it came from a very big animal. It was not a very sharp tooth, so he knew the animal ate plants, not meat. And it looked different from the teeth of almost every animal alive today. The only living animal with teeth like that was the big lizard called an iguana. So Dr Mantell called it *Iguanodon*. Later, when he found some more bones, he learned more about its legs, arms, and head.

Dinosaur footprints in Alberta, Canada

In the same way, when William Buckland found *Megalosaurus*, he knew that it *was* a meat-eater, because of its sharp teeth.

Trace fossils are things like dinosaur footprints, eggs, and dung. Dinosaur footprints can tell us how it walked. Did it walk on two feet or four? How fast could it run? The footprints of one theropod from Texas show that it was running at 39 kilometres per hour, faster than a horse!

The eggs and nests tell us about dinosaur babies and family life. And dinosaur dung? Yes, scientists look at this carefully too. When they find bits of plants or animals in it, they know what the dinosaur was eating. (The dung is millions of years old, and has become hard like rock, so it does not smell bad.)

Today, scientists use computers to make pictures of dinosaur bones, to see how they worked. They can watch the dinosaurs moving on the computer.

How do we know that meat-eaters like *Tyrannosaurus rex* killed other dinosaurs? The scientist Robert Bakker answers that. He calls himself a murder detective. Dinosaur scientists, he says, 'dig up murder victims from 144 million years ago. Then we figure out who killed them.' How does he do that? He looks for 'bullets' and 'bullet wounds'. The 'bullets' are dinosaur teeth. Meat-eating dinosaurs often lost one or two teeth when they killed, or were eating, other dinosaurs. They grew new ones later. So when Bakker finds teeth near a dead diplodocus, it is like finding a bullet near a dead man. If he finds allosaur teeth, he knows that an allosaur was the killer.

And when he finds tooth damage on bones, the damage is like 'bullet wounds'. It also gives him information about the killer.

Robert Bakker with an allosaur jaw

Were dinosaurs cold-blooded, like lizards and fish, or warm-blooded, like mammals? Cold-blooded animals do not need much food, and move slowly when it is cold. Warm-blooded animals need much more food, and move quickly, even in cold weather.

Lizards are cold-blooded, and until the 1970s scientists thought that dinosaurs were big lizards. But today, most scientists think that dinosaurs were warm-blooded. John Ostrom thinks *Deinonychus* was warm-blooded, because it could move so quickly. And some dinosaurs lived in Antarctica, which was not always warm even in the Cretaceous. We know that dinosaurs grew very quickly too, and cold-blooded animals do not do that. So most dinosaurs were probably warm-blooded, like us.

But there are plenty of things we do not know. What type of noise did *Parasaurolophus* make? Did it really sing? Lots of dinosaurs probably made noises, but nobody has ever heard them.

And what colour were dinosaurs? Again, nobody knows, because colour does not stay in fossils. But dinosaurs were probably colourful, like birds and animals today. Think of the large frills on the heads of *Protoceratops* and *Triceratops*, or the 'hat' on *Lambeosaurus*. They were probably there to frighten enemies, and to attract females. And a brightly coloured frill is much easier to see.

Lots of birds today are brightly coloured. And many dinosaurs, like birds, had feathers. So lots of dinosaurs were probably covered with beautiful feathers, just like birds. But what colour were they?

Nobody knows.

11 Dinosaurs today

In 1896, the rich Scottish-American businessman Andrew Carnegie built a Museum of Natural History in Pittsburgh, Pennsylvania. Carnegie wanted the biggest dinosaur in the world for his museum, so he asked his scientists to find one. At Sheep Creek, near the Freezeout Mountains in Wyoming, they found what they wanted – an enormous diplodocus. At that time, it was the biggest dinosaur in the world. They called it *Diplodocus carnegii*, giving it Carnegie's name. Carnegie was very happy. But he had a problem: his museum was not big enough. So he had to build a huge, new room, just to keep his diplodocus in.

When King Edward the Seventh of England visited Carnegie at his castle in Scotland, he saw a picture of Carnegie's diplodocus.

'I say, Carnegie, what in the world is this?' the king asked.

Carnegie smiled and told him that it was the biggest animal that ever lived – and that it had Carnegie's name.

'Oh! I say, Carnegie,' the king said. 'We must have one of these in the British Museum.'

Carnegie loved to be important, so in 1905, he sent a model of his diplodocus to the Natural History Museum in London. Later, he sent models to museums in Berlin, Paris, Vienna, Bologna, St Petersburg, Buenos Aires, Madrid, Mexico City, and Munich.

Carnegie's diplodocus is one of the most popular dinosaurs in the world. Millions of people see it every year, all over the world. In London, the diplodocus is called

Andrew Carnegie

Dippy arrives in 1905

'Dippy.' Children sometimes spend the night in the Natural History Museum, sleeping under Dippy and learning about other dinosaurs.

In Carnegie's Pittsburgh Museum, there is a tyrannosaurus rex called 'Samson'. Children love that too. It is fun to sleep under a diplodocus, or to stand in front of a tyrannosaurus like Samson in a museum. There are many other museums with dinosaurs to see too. Some of the best are the Field Museum in Chicago, the American Museum of Natural History in New York, the Natural History Museum in Beijing, and the Royal Tyrrell Museum in Alberta, Canada.

If you cannot see a real dinosaur, you can still play with one on your computer. And you can have fun with dinosaur games too. Dinosaurs have appeared in hundreds of computer games since 1986. In 1990, a likeable green dinosaur called 'Yoshi' appeared in the computer game *Super Mario World* – he soon became famous, and even had his own games. But with their sharp teeth and claws, and enormous bodies, dinosaurs are more often seen in fighting games. Since 1997, millions of people have enjoyed fighting dangerous dinosaurs in the seven very successful *Turok* games. And in the last five years, dinosaur games have become even more popular, with new games like *Dino Run*, *Dino D-Day* and *Velociraptor Safari*.

But can you imagine a world with dinosaurs and humans together? In the 1900s, people began to write books about this idea. One of the first was *The Lost World* by Sir Arthur Conan Doyle. In this book, a scientist called Professor Challenger discovers dinosaurs still living on a mountain in South America.

More recently, Michael Crichton's book *Jurassic Park* – later a popular film by Steven Spielberg – uses the same idea. In this book, scientists find dinosaur blood in the stomach of a fossilized insect. They use this blood to make new dinosaurs.

Jurassic Park – the film

Is this really possible? Scientists say no – well, not yet. And that is a good thing. After all, dinosaurs are much, much bigger than us. If we bring back dinosaurs, we will not be able to talk to them, or make friends with them. And when a tyrannosaur sees a human, it will think just one thing – lunch!

Remember, birds are dinosaurs. *Tyrannosaurus* was, in some ways, like an enormous chicken. So if you want to see a real living dinosaur, watch a group of hungry chickens eating their food. Then think of a chicken as big as a house.

Do you really want the dinosaurs to come back?

GLOSSARY

archosaur a very early kind of dinosaur

attract to make somebody like something

bear a big wild animal with thick fur

bone one of the hard white parts inside the body of an animal; (*adj*) **bony**

brain the part of the head that thinks and remembers

breathe to take air in through your nose or mouth

club a heavy stick with one thick end, used as a weapon

cold-blooded having a body temperature that changes as the air or water temperature changes

continent a very large area of land, e.g. Africa

crocodile a big animal with a long tail and a big mouth with sharp teeth

defend to fight to keep away things that attack

dung solid waste from animals

Earth the world

elephant a very big wild animal from Africa or Asia, with a long nose that hangs down

enormous very big

evolve to change slowly over time

female belonging to the sex that can have babies

fossil part of a dead plant or animal that has changed to rock over a long time; (*v*) **fossilize** to become a fossil

herd a big group of animals of the same kind

hollow with an empty space inside

huge very big

human a person, not an animal or machine

hunt to chase animals and kill them

iguana a large American lizard

imagine to make a picture of something in your mind

insect a very small animal that has six legs

jaw one of the two bones in the head that hold the teeth

lay (past tense **laid**) to bring an egg out of the body

lion   a large wild animal of the cat family

lizard   a small animal that has four legs and a long tail

male   belonging to the sex that cannot have babies

mammal   an animal that drinks milk from its mother's body
   when it is young

model   a copy of something

mouse   a small animal with a long tail

museum   a place where you can look at old or interesting things

nest   a place where a bird or snake keeps its eggs and its babies

ornithiscian   a plant-eating dinosaur with very thick skin

period   an amount of time

rhinoceros   a big animal with thick skin and a horn on its nose

sand   very small pieces of rock that you find on beaches

sauropod   a big plant-eating dinosaur with a long neck and tail

scientist   a person who studies natural things

sharp   with a point that cuts or makes holes easily

snake   an animal with a long thin body and no legs

theropod   a meat-eating dinosaur

up to   as much as or as many as

victim   someone who suffers as the result of a crime

volcano   a mountain with a hole in the top where fire and gas
   sometimes come out

warm-blooded   having a body temperature that does not change
   when the air or water temperature changes

weight   how heavy something is; (*v*) **weigh**

wound   a hurt place in the body

INDEX

Numbers in **bold** are for pictures

Dinosaurs

ACTIVITIES

ACTIVITIES

Before Reading

1 What do you know about dinosaurs? Circle *a*, *b* or *c*.

1 The word 'dinosaur' was first used in _____.
   a) 1786   b) 1842   c) 1898

2 There are _____ main groups of dinosaurs.
   a) three   b) five   c) six

3 Dinosaurs lived _____ humans.
   a) before   b) after   c) at the same time as

4 Dinosaurs disappeared because of _____.
   a) an earthquake   b) a meteor   c) a fire

5 The last dinosaurs lived _____ million years ago.
   a) 230   b) 165   c) 65

6 Scientists now think that _____ evolved from dinosaurs.
   a) dogs   b) humans   c) birds

2 Three of these sentences are correct. Which ones are they?

1 Dippy is a dinosaur in the Natural History Museum in London, England.

2 When the Atlantic Ocean appeared in the Jurassic period, it was about 200 kilometres wide.

3 Some dinosaurs had up to 720 teeth.

4 Some dinosaurs had feathers, but none of them could fly.

5 A meteor that landed in China meant the end for the dinosaurs.

6 Scientists think that dinosaurs were probably warm-blooded.

ACTIVITIES

While Reading

Read Chapter 1. Then fill the gaps with these names.

Joseph Anning, Mary Anning, William Buckland,
Edward Drinker Cope, Gideon Mantell, Othniel C. Marsh,
Richard Owen

1 _____ found the first ichthyosaur fossil.
2 _____ helped his sister to find fossils.
3 _____ ate all kinds of dead animals.
4 _____ studied a tooth and bones for three years.
5 _____ cut up a dead rhinoceros.
6 _____ was the winner in the Bone Wars.
7 _____ discovered fifty-six kinds of dinosaur.

Read Chapters 2 and 3. Then circle the correct words.

1 *Sauroposeidon* was the *longest / tallest* dinosaur.
2 Modern humans have been on Earth for *more / less* than 200,000 years.
3 The first dinosaurs moved on *two / four* legs.
4 *Pterosaurs / Plesiosaurs* lived in the sea.
5 Modern scientists think that Owen's idea of three groups of dinosaurs is *right / wrong*.
6 *Coelophysis* could move fast because its bones were not *short / heavy*.
7 *Thecodontosaurus* ate *plants / fish*.
8 The first dinosaur that was found outside England was in *Germany / Argentina*.
9 The ornithiscians appeared *before / after* the sauropods.

Read Chapter 4, then match these halves of sentences.

1 Sauropods had very heavy bodies . . .
2 Sauropods could lift their long necks easily . . .
3 *Brachiosaurus* was different from most dinosaurs . . .
4 Because there was plenty of food to eat . . .
5 Scientists know that *Allosaurus* was a successful killer . . .
6 *Ceratosaurus* hunted for its food . . .
7 Plesiosaurs used their big flat hands . . .
8 Many pterodactyls were as big as large birds . . .

a because some of the bones were hollow.
b because it changed very little over 100 million years.
c but their mouths were full of sharp teeth.
d to push themselves through the water.
e so they walked on all four feet.
f dinosaurs got much bigger in the Jurassic period.
g both on land and in the water.
h because its back legs were shorter than its front legs.

Read Chapter 5. Are these sentences true (T) or false (F)?
Rewrite the false ones with the correct information.

1 Large sauropods were found on every continent.
2 Scientists think that *Deinonychus* hunted alone.
3 We know that *Baryonyx* ate meat and fish, because
   scientists found a lot of bones near its body.
4 *Tyrannosaurus rex* had arms that were unusually small.
5 Tyrannosaurs ate dead animals and hunted living ones too.
6 *Velociraptor* ran very fast on four legs.
7 The protoceratops and the velociraptor were hunting
   together when they died.

Read Chapter 6 and answer the questions.

1 What did ornithiscians use to defend themselves?
2 What was the frill on *Protoceratops* used for?
3 How do we know that *Stegosaurus* used its tail as
  a weapon?
4 What useful weapon did *Ankylosaurus* have?
5 What was different about the way *Iguanodon* ate?
6 What happened when a hadrosaur lost a tooth?
7 What was the 'hat' on *Lambeosaurus* made of?
8 What happened when scientists blew air into the hollow
  bone from a parasaurolophus?

Read Chapters 7 and 8, then circle *a*, *b* or *c*.

1 When she died, the oviraptor was _____ her eggs.
  a) taking care of   b) eating   c) stealing
2 *Maiasaura* brought _____ to her children.
  a) eggs   b) plants   c) bones.
3 Scientists know that maiasaurs were _____-blooded.
  a) hot   b) cold   c) warm
4 The fastest tyrannosaurs were the _____.
  a) babies   b) children   c) adults
5 Huxley noticed that *Archaeopteryx* had _____ bones.
  a) short   b) heavy   c) hollow
6 The _____ showed that *Sinosauropteryx* had had feathers.
  a) bones   b) sand   c) light
7 It is possible that *Microraptor* flew with _____.
  a) four wings   b) one tail   c) no feathers
8 Dinosaurs possibly learned to fly after they began to
  climb _____.
  a) trees   b) plants   c) rocks

Read Chapter 9. Fill in the gaps with these words.

clay, crater, mammal, meat-eaters, meteor, plant-eaters,
warmer

1 In the time of the dinosaurs, Antarctica was much _____
   than it is today.
2 Where Cretaceous rocks meet Tertiary rocks, there is a line
   of _____ called iridium.
3 Alvarez realized that the iridium came from a huge _____.
4 The _____ died before the _____.
5 Nobody could see the _____, because it was under the
   ground.
6 Among the animals that lived after the meteor arrived there
   was an early _____.

Read Chapters 10 and 11. Rewrite these untrue sentences
with the correct information.

1 Scientists usually find all the bones of a dinosaur together.
2 Plant-eaters have very sharp teeth.
3 Dung is an example of a body fossil.
4 Robert Bakker says that he is a murder victim.
5 Scientists now think that most dinosaurs were probably
   cold-blooded.
6 King Edward the Seventh sent a model of a dinosaur to the
   Natural History Museum.
7 Children can sometimes ride Dippy the dinosaur at the
   Natural History Museum.
8 Now you can watch dangerous dinosaurs singing in
   computer games.
9 Scientists can make new dinosaurs from the blood of living
   dinosaurs.

ACTIVITIES

After Reading

1 Use the clues below to complete the puzzle. Then find the hidden nine-letter word.

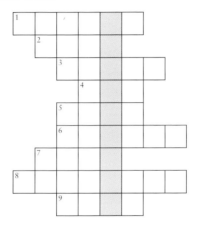

1 A dinosaur egg is an example of a trace _____.
2 Solid waste from animals.
3 A hurt place in the body.
4 An animal's teeth are held in this.
5 One of the hard white parts inside an animal.
6 To change very slowly over time.
7 A big group of animals of the same kind.
8 *Baryonyx* was this kind of dinosaur.
9 To chase and kill animals.

The hidden word is _____.

2 Perhaps this is what some of the people in the book are thinking. Who are they? What is happening/has just happened?

1 'I've won! I've got twenty-four more than him. It's taken a long time, and it's been a hard fight. But now everyone in America must agree – I'm the best dinosaur hunter.'

2 'Of course we couldn't see it. It's under the ground! Why didn't I think of that before? This means my idea was right – it was a meteor that brought the end of the dinosaurs.'

3 'There – I think everything is ready now. Well, it's going to be a night that they will all remember. Anybody can have a dinner party, but a dinner party inside an iguanodon – that's something special!'

4 'Am I pleased? Of course I'm pleased. I've got a dinosaur that's named after me. And now the king wants a copy of it. The king! And of course he shall have one – or the museum shall. I don't suppose that the king wants to wake up every morning and see a dinosaur looking at him.'

5 'Well, I've thought about it for a long time now, and now I'm ready for the whole world to know about it. This paper will tell everybody about this extraordinary animal. I'm going to name it after the iguana because of its teeth.'

3 One word in each group (1–4) does not belong there. Which is it? Then choose the best headings for each group from this list.

birds, dinosaurs, large animals, sharp body parts

1 _____: crocodile, elephant, mouse, rhinoceros
2 _____: human, ornithiscian, sauropod, theropod
3 _____: beak, brain, claw, spike
4 _____: egg, feather, mammal, nest

4 **Do you agree or disagree with these statements? Why?**

1 There are more important things to spend money on than old bones.
2 It is important to learn about our past and the history of life on our planet.
3 It is not right to make books and films about dinosaurs that are different from real life dinosaurs.
4 Everybody should see real dinosaur fossils once in their life.

5 **What is your favourite dinosaur? Find some information about it and make a poster or give a short talk to your class. Think about these questions.**

- When did it live?
- What did it look like, and what was special about it?
- Where can you see fossils from this dinosaur?

These websites can help you:

http://www.enchantedlearning.com/subjects/dinosaurs/
http://science.nationalgeographic.com/science/
    prehistoric-world.html
http://paleobiology.si.edu/dinosaurs/

ABOUT THE AUTHOR

Tim Vicary was born in London, but he spent a lot of his childhood near the sea, in Devon, in the south-west of England. As a boy, he had lots of animals at home – horses, dogs, cats, and rabbits – and he sometimes went looking for fossils on the beach at Lyme Regis, just like Mary Anning.

He went to Cambridge University, worked as a schoolteacher, and is now a teaching fellow at the Norwegian Study Centre at the University of York. He is married, has two children, and lives in the country in Yorkshire, in the north of England. He still has lots of animals at home.

He has written about 20 books for Oxford Bookworms, from Starter to Stage 3. His other Oxford Bookworms titles at Stage 3 are *The Brontë Story* (True Stories), *Chemical Secret* (Thriller and Adventure), *The Everest Story* (Factfiles), *Justice* (Thriller and Adventure), *The Mysterious Death of Charles Bravo* (True Stories) and *Skyjack!* (Thriller and Adventure). *The Everest Story* was the winner of the Extensive Reading Foundation's Language Literature Award in the Adolescents and Adults Intermediate category in 2011. *Titanic* (Factfiles Stage 1) won the Award in the Adolescents and Adults Elementary category in 2010.

Tim has written three crime novels, about a tough lady lawyer called Sarah Newby. These are: *A Game of Proof*, *Fatal Verdict*, and *Bold Counsel*. He has also written two romantic historical novels: *The Blood Upon the Rose*, and *Cat and Mouse*. All these books are published as e-books for Amazon Kindle.

You can read more about Tim and his books on his website, www.timvicary.com

OXFORD BOOKWORMS LIBRARY

Classics • Crime & Mystery • Factfiles • Fantasy & Horror
Human Interest • Playscripts • Thriller & Adventure
True Stories • World Stories

The OXFORD BOOKWORMS LIBRARY provides enjoyable reading in English, with a wide range of classic and modern fiction, non-fiction, and plays. It includes original and adapted texts in seven carefully graded language stages, which take learners from beginner to advanced level. An overview is given on the next pages.

All Stage 1 titles are available as audio recordings, as well as over eighty other titles from Starter to Stage 6. All Starters and many titles at Stages 1 to 4 are specially recommended for younger learners. Every Bookworm is illustrated, and Starters and Factfiles have full-colour illustrations.

The OXFORD BOOKWORMS LIBRARY also offers extensive support. Each book contains an introduction to the story, notes about the author, a glossary, and activities. Additional resources include tests and worksheets, and answers for these and for the activities in the books. There is advice on running a class library, using audio recordings, and the many ways of using Oxford Bookworms in reading programmes. Resource materials are available on the website <www.oup.com/bookworms>.

The *Oxford Bookworms Collection* is a series for advanced learners. It consists of volumes of short stories by well-known authors, both classic and modern. Texts are not abridged or adapted in any way, but carefully selected to be accessible to the advanced student.

You can find details and a full list of titles in the *Oxford Bookworms Library Catalogue* and *Oxford English Language Teaching Catalogues*, and on the website <www.oup.com/bookworms>.

THE OXFORD BOOKWORMS LIBRARY
GRADING AND SAMPLE EXTRACTS

STARTER • 250 HEADWORDS

present simple – present continuous – imperative –
can/cannot, must – going to (future) – simple gerunds …

Her phone is ringing – but where is it?

Sally gets out of bed and looks in her bag. No phone.
She looks under the bed. No phone. Then she looks behind
the door. There is her phone. Sally picks up her phone and
answers it. *Sally's Phone*

STAGE 1 • 400 HEADWORDS

… past simple – coordination with *and*, *but*, *or* –
subordination with *before*, *after*, *when*, *because*, *so* …

I knew him in Persia. He was a famous builder and I
worked with him there. For a time I was his friend, but
not for long. When he came to Paris, I came after him –
I wanted to watch him. He was a very clever, very
dangerous man. *The Phantom of the Opera*

STAGE 2 • 700 HEADWORDS

… present perfect – *will* (future) – *(don't) have to, must not, could* –
comparison of adjectives – simple *if* clauses – past continuous –
tag questions – *ask/tell* + infinitive …

While I was writing these words in my diary, I decided
what to do. I must try to escape. I shall try to get down the
wall outside. The window is high above the ground, but
I have to try. I shall take some of the gold with me – if I
escape, perhaps it will be helpful later. *Dracula*

STAGE 3 • 1000 HEADWORDS
… should, may – present perfect continuous – *used to* – past perfect –
causative – relative clauses – indirect statements …

Of course, it was most important that no one should see
Colin, Mary, or Dickon entering the secret garden. So Colin
gave orders to the gardeners that they must all keep away
from that part of the garden in future. *The Secret Garden*

STAGE 4 • 1400 HEADWORDS
… past perfect continuous – passive (simple forms) –
would conditional clauses – indirect questions –
relatives with *where/when* – gerunds after prepositions/phrases …

I was glad. Now Hyde could not show his face to the world
again. If he did, every honest man in London would be proud
to report him to the police. *Dr Jekyll and Mr Hyde*

STAGE 5 • 1800 HEADWORDS
… future continuous – future perfect –
passive (modals, continuous forms) –
would have conditional clauses – modals + perfect infinitive …

If he had spoken Estella's name, I would have hit him. I was so
angry with him, and so depressed about my future, that I could
not eat the breakfast. Instead I went straight to the old house.
Great Expectations

STAGE 6 • 2500 HEADWORDS
… passive (infinitives, gerunds) – advanced modal meanings –
clauses of concession, condition

When I stepped up to the piano, I was confident. It was as if I
knew that the prodigy side of me really did exist. And when I
started to play, I was so caught up in how lovely I looked that
I didn't worry how I would sound. *The Joy Luck Club*

BOOKWORMS · FACTFILES · STAGE 3

The Everest Story

TIM VICARY

It is beautiful to look at, hard to reach, and terribly difficult to climb. Winds of 200 kilometres per hour or more scream across it day and night, while the temperature falls to -20 °C or lower. Every year, some who try to climb the highest mountain in the world do not return.

But for a century people have been coming to climb Everest – some alone, some in groups, but all with a dream of going to the highest place in the world. This is their story.

BOOKWORMS · FACTFILES · STAGE 3

Future Energy

ALEX RAYNHAM

Right now, all over the world, people are using energy. As we drive our cars, work on our computers, or even cook food on a wood fire, we probably do not stop to think about where the energy comes from. But when the gas is gone and there is no more coal – what then?

Scientists are finding new answers all the time. Get ready for the children whose running feet make the energy to bring water to their village; for the power station that uses warm and cold water to make energy; for the car that saves energy by growing like a plant . . .